# Contents

# Introduction

From the invasion of Britain to the siege of Paris, the Viking age is indeed one of the most tumultuous and formative periods of European history. But what of the forces behind the seismic raids and explorations? What of the ingenious craftsmanship behind the longboats that were beyond their time? Often, a farrago of myths and facts continues to portray a rather foggy image of the Vikings; but could the Vikings truly be the savage seafarers that history condemns them to be?

This book provides a balanced and riveting account of the Viking age—from its dawn to dusk. Without white washing the savagery of the Vikings, it chronicles the many raids that were undertaken. It also presents another view point of these fascinating people. Employing the latest archeological finds and various sources, it paints a different yet factual picture of the Vikings. The book delves into the many cultural aspects of the society: religion—the Nordic gods—social structure, cloth, house and much besides.

Their celebrated ship architecture is discussed at length, myths are debunked, legends are deliberated—many facets of this epoch are dilated in detail.

# Who Were the Vikings?

The Vikings are known by different names: the Anglo-Saxon knew them as Dene (Danes); the Germans, Ascomanni, ashmen; the Slaves, Arabs and Byzantines, Rus' or Rhos. But Viking is a generic term used to refer to the Scandinavians from Sweden, Denmark, and Norway of the Viking era.

Phenomenal seafaring warriors, the Vikings raided, traded, explored and settled across large parts of Europe. They also made inroads as distant as Russia, Constantinople and North America. The Vikings knew no bounds in their ventures to places hitherto unknown to them.

Their unmatched skills in coordinately carrying out their marauding expeditions notwithstanding, the Vikings were not professional privateers or soldiers. Indeed, most of them were farmers and fishermen who would only embark on these expeditions in the summer after the summoning of their local leaders.

Continue to read to discover the fascinating culture of these legendary people in the latter chapters.

# The Viking Age

The Viking Age is the era in the history of Europe, particularly Northern Europe and Scandinavia, which was from A.D.793–1066. This is the epoch when Norsemen hailing from Scandinavian traveled through Europe for the purpose of trade, invasion, and conquest. Several historical documents propose various catalysts for the invasion of the

Vikings.Retribution in response to the aggression of Christians towards the pagan people, overpopulation, deficiency of sustainable farmland in their native countyand trade inequities are believed to have been factors.

Considered to be ferocious pirates, the seafaring Normans were great explorers and travelers. They established their lives in present-day Faroe Islands, England, Ireland, Newfoundland, Scotland, Iceland, Normandy, Anatolia, Norse Greenland and Ukraine.

The Vikings also made a journey east to Russia and settled in many places there including the Baltic states of Estonia, Lithuania and Latvia. Additionally, they traveled to the Arabian world in northern Africa: Algeria, Morocco, and Tunisia. There were actually over two million Arabian coins recovered in Viking burials ubiquitously in Scandinavia.

Early on in the Viking Age, the knowledge of coinage in Scandinavia was slight. But due to trading contact with both Western Europe and the Islamic world to the east, foreign coins came in the region.

Apart from chief trading ports during the time such as Hedeby and Ribe, however, the idea of coinage in Denmark was unknown. It was only in terms of weight in silver or gold coins were valued and distributed alongside several other forms of precious metal.

The main basis to adopting coinage was probably political, cultural as well as economic. Similar to other invaders, the Vikings, in observing the civilized people under their reign, desired to resemble them.

## Probable grounds of Norse enlargement

In the eighth century, the Vikings hailing from Norway, Sweden and Denmark, began to construct and dispatch warships purposed to ransack various destinations. This instigated the Viking age. Travelers of The North Sea were traders, explorers, colonizers and also pillagers.

The motive behind the Viking expansion still remains a debatable topic in Nordic history.

According to one common theory posited by historians, during the time Charlemagne was in power, via the use of coercion and terror, pagans were forced to proselytize into Christians. This eventuated in Vikings and other pagans' resort to retaliation. Professor Rudolf Simek argues

*"it is not a coincidence if the early Viking activity occurred during the reign of Charlemagne."*

The spread of Christianity in Scandinavia triggered serious conflict which brought about a division in Norway that was to last for nearly a century.

Another explanation for the Viking expansion is trade. The desire for goods led the Scandinavian traders to travel and advance large trading partnership in new territories. It has been indicated that the trade practices imposed by Christianity was ultimately the reason that the commerce of Scandinavians was corrupted.

Other historians argue that the Scandinavian migration was because of the infertile farmland that was not enough to furnish the needs of the growing population of the peninsula.

## Historical Overview

A.D. 787 is given as the earliest date of a Viking incursion (*Anglo-Saxon Chronicle* however dates it A.D 787 instead of A.D. 789) when, in accord with *Anglo-SaxonChronicle*, a clutch of Norwegian soldiers cruised to Dorset. There, the royal officials mistook the Vikings for merchants. They slew him without delay as he endeavored to escort them to the King's manor to disburse tax for their goods.

In Britain, The dawn of the Viking age is, nevertheless, marked as A.D. 793. A record in the *Anglo-Saxon Chronicle* indicates that the monastery of Lindisfarne was invaded by the Northmen.

> *"A.D. 793. This year came dreadful fore-warnings over the land of the*

*Northumbrians, terrifying the people most woefully: these were immense sheets of light rushing through the air, and whirlwinds, and fiery dragons flying across the firmament. These tremendous tokens were soon followed by a great famine: and not long after, on the sixth day before the ides of January in the same year, the harrowing inroads of heathen men made lamentable havoc in the church of God in Holy-island (Lindisfarne), by rapine and slaughter.*

*— Anglo Saxon Chronicle."*

In accordance with the *Annals of Ulster*, there was a grave incursion on Lindisfarne's mother-house of Iona in 795. The Norsemen, from the footholds there, descended on Iona once more, ensuing massacre amongst the CèliDè Brethren, and setting the abbey on fire in 802.

## The End of the Viking Age

In England, the conclusion of the Viking's presence is normally denoted by the unsuccessful raid endeavored by the King of Norway, Harald III. He was overcome by Harold Godwinson, Saxon King, at the Battle of Stamford Bridge in 1066. In Ireland, the end of the Vikings was marked by the siege of Dublin by Strongbow along with the help of his Hiberno-Norman armies in 1171. And in Scotland, King HákonHákonarson's defeat at the Battle of Largs in 1263 concluded the Viking age.

Within a month, Godwinson was later defeated by another Viking, William, who was the Duke of Normandy (a nation that was captured by Vikings in 911).

The Viking era, in Scandinavia, is deemed to have terminated in the early eleventh century following the formation of royal force and the prevalence of Christianity as the main religion in Scandinavia.

The reign of King OlovSkötkonung (appr. 995-1020), in Sweden, is believed to have marked the shift from the Viking era to the Middle Ages. He was the first king of Sweden that was Christian.

# The Raids and Settlements of the Vikings

## England

### The Vikings arrive

It was in the year A.D. 789 the three ships of the Viking arrived in Dorset, on the Isle of Portland. Assuming they were merchants the Reeve of Dorchester, the King's officer, took with him some of his men to the harbor. He commanded the transport of the seafarers to the King's town; however, the officer and his men were promptly slaughtered. This was the one of the first records of the Viking raid.  The incursion, nevertheless, is believed to be more of a gone wrong trading expedition than a practical one.

## Massacre at the Lindisfarne Monastery

On January 793, the largely unguarded monastic site in Lindisfarne, otherwise known as Holy Island, was unexpectedly struck by the powerful navy of Vikings from Denmark. They ransacked the area and other buildings, slaughtered several of the monks, seized treasures, devoured the cattle, and much besides. The incursion marks the commencement of the "Viking Age of Invasion", made successful by the Viking longship. Small-scaled raids continued across coastal England. While the first attacking units were minimal, it is believed that the incursion was engineered meticulously. They carried out their attacks during the coldest day of winter knowing there would be no accessible support from the coast.

It wasn't long after that the information of the raid began to disseminate all around Europe. The Northumbrian scholar Alcuin of York wrote to the Higbald, the bishop of Lindisfarne and to Ethelred, King of Northumbria, bewailing the unforeseen Viking damage of the Holy Island in Northumbria:

> *"Lo, it is almost three hundred and fifty years that we and our forefathers have*

*dwelt in this fair land, and never has such a horror before appeared in Englaland, such as we have just suffered from the heathen. It was not thought possible that they cloud have made such a voyage. Behold the church of St Cuthbert sprinkled with the blood of the priests of Christ, robbed of all its ornaments....In that place where, after the departure of Paulinus from York, the Christian faith had its beginning among us, there is the beginning of woe and calamity.....Portents of this woe came before it.....What signifies that rain of blood during Lent in the town of York?"*

---

Several religious foundations in the north were demolished over the next few decades.

The forays of the Vikings in England were sporadic until the 840s. The Norwegians conducted their invasion during the winter of 840 and 841, instead of the summer. In Kent, the Vikings, in 850, for the first time overwintered in England. And in the 860s, they started to amass larger armies with the clear intention of conquest.

The Great Heathen Army spearheaded by the Brothers Ivar the Boneless (the architect behind the Scandinavian invasion of England), Hálfdan and Ubba, as well as Guthrum, another Viking, landed in East Anglia. The Vikings coerced the East Angles to help supply an army and in A.D. 866 seized York. In A.D. 867 they annexed southern Northumbria.

Alfred of Wessex, the only English king to be called "the Great", was able to keep the Vikings beyond the borders of Wessex. Notably, he hid in the woods and marshes near Athelney (Somerset) in 878 AD, covertly assembling his scattered warriors from all over the west of England. Alfred finally emerged with his restructured army and defeated the Vikings later that year at Edington (Wiltshire).

Despite the fact that king Alfred of Wessex succeeded in overcoming the Danish Vikings, he came to realize that his army could not force all the Vikings out of England. He then decided to reach conformity with the Vikings which enabled them to dwell in the eastern and western part of England called Danelaw.
Alfred, including his successors, managed to keep the Viking at bay and reclaim York. There was an emergence of new Vikings from Norway in England in A.D. 947 when Eric Bloodaxe seized York.

The Danish King Sweyn Forkbeard, in 1003, began a succession of attack against England. This ended up in a complete incursion which eventuated in Sweyn assuming the throne of England in 1013. He was simultaneously the king of Denmark and some parts of Norway. After the death of Sweyn in 1014, Edmund Ironside of Wessex claimed the throne of England. Sweyn's son, Canute (or Cnut), won back the throne of England in A.D. 1016 by way of conquest. During his reign of more than twenty years, Canute was a strong King who governed sensibly. He introduced some Danish customs to England, and also appointed many Englishmen as bishops in Denmark. Cnut died in 1035. He was known as the king of Norway, England, Denmark and some areas of Sweden.

The end of the Viking age was marked when Harold II, the last Anglo-Saxon king of England, won the Battle of Stamford Bridge on 25th September 1066. Even though he successfully repelled the invaders led by Harald Hardrada of Norway in the bloody and horrific battle, his victory was ephemeral.

Three weeks later, the armies of William of Normandy and Harold had a battle near Hastings on the south coast of England on 14th October 1066. After a lengthy and exhaustive battle, Harold was murdered and his army defeated by William of Normandy at the Battle of Hastings.

## Scotland

There is scarcity of written material, but it's known that the first raid of the Vikings in Scotland is dated 794 on Iona's holy island.

A massive Norse navy raided the River Earn and River Tay in 839, which were both very navigable. They landed in the center of the Pictish kingdom. The Vikings defeated Eogán mac Óengusa, the king of the Picts and Bran, his brother, the king of the Scots.

The kingdom which was sophisticatedly established collapsed, together with the leadership of the Picts, which sustained its stability for over a century.

The Norsemen, by the mid ninth century, had settled in Orkney, the Hebrides and Man, Shetland and other areas of Scotland. In some measure, the Norsemen were fusing themselves with the Gaelic society in the Hebrides and Man. The local Jarls were the rulers of these areas. The Jarl of Shetland and Orkney, nevertheless, asserted supremacy.

King Harald Fairhair, in 875, led an army from Scotland to Norway. In his endeavour to amalgamate Norway, he discovered that many of those who contested to his ascension to the throne had fled to the Isles. From there, they were attacking Norway. He arranged a force that was able to subjugate dissidents, which had the Jarls, who were independent, under his rule. He ended up governing Norway, Man, the Isles, and other areas of Scotland.

In Scotland, it is deemed that the Viking age came to an end in 1266. The Norwegian king, Haakon IV, sent his fleets from Orkney and Norway to west coast in 1263. It was in retribution for the expedition of the Scots to Skye. His fleet joined with those of King Dougal of the Hebrides and King Magnus of Man. When Haakon refused to cede the Isles to Scotland through negotiations, and decided instead to invade, this ended up causing the Battle of Largs in 1263. And in July 1266 a treat was prepared, *"Treaty of Perth"*, ceding the Isles and Kingdom of Man along with all of Scotland's regions to Alexander III.

## Ireland
### Intensive raid and settlement in Ireland
The first recorded Viking raid in the Irish history was in 795 when they plundered the monasteries on Rathlin Island, where the church was burned. On Inismurray and Inisbofin the monasteries situated on the west coast were sacked possibly by the same raiders. It was the same year that the Scottish island of Iona was attacked. These raiders are believed to be exclusively from Norway.

The Vikings carried out an extensive depredation in Ireland. In 812, they founded Limerick, where they built their own town next to Waterford in 853. The Vikings invaded Dubhlinn (present day Dublin), and asserted their power until 1169. During this period, they also founded trading ports in Cork.

The Viking raids on Ireland became more intense from 830, and exacerbated during the following decades. In 832, for instance, there was extensive pillaging in the lands of the Cianachta near the sea in Louth. The Vikings raided the land of UíNéill of southern Brega in 836, and attacked the lands of Connacht. A fleet of sixty ships emerged on the Boyne and a similar fleet on the Liffey in 837. After a while, the Vikings made their way up Shannon and the Erne and put a fleet on Lough Neagh.

In 840-41, the Vikings for the first time wintered on Lough Neagh. They established a longphort at Annagassan in Louth and at Dubhlinn and employed these bases for attacks on the south and west.

The most important settlement in the long term was Dubhlinn, as by the mid 9th century, there was a booming community of Norsemen. In the British Isles, this community became the chief trader of slaves. They also traded in Irish markets in Dubhlinn. Imported fabrics from England, Persia, Byzantine and central Asia were founded during excavations.

With the Irish, the Vikings began to intermix. They even began to establish partnerships and matrimonial relationships. Many settlements of the Vikings, meanwhile, turned into towns. Dubhlinn, in time, flourished as a merchant town until an Irish attack in 902 brought it to its ruins. The Vikings' power base was later transported to the Isle of Man and to the expanding territory. Other Viking towns such as Cork, Vadrefjord (Waterford), and Youghàl were also overcome.

The Vikings, however, recaptured the settlement of Vadrefjord (914) and the settlement of Dubhlinn (917), which the Irish had captured in 902, in the 2nd round of the Viking attacks on Ireland.

**Battle of Clontarf**
The Battle of Clontarf, in 1014, 23rd April was the last major battle that involved the Vikings. This was the event in which the Vikings battled for both Viking-led army rivals and the Irish over King Brian Boru's army. The Battle which lasted from sunrise to sunset was a portentous event in Irish history. This battle signaled the weakening of the Norse Dublin and the effective conclusion of the Vikings in Ireland. The Battle of Clontarf is often depicted in Irish and Viking literature as the assembly of the natural and the supernatural: demons, goblins and witches.

# Iceland
The chronicles of Iceland dates back to the late 800s, following the settlement of the Vikings and those they had enslaved. The common date of settlement in Iceland is 874 AD; however, archeological evidence designates that prior

to the coming of the Vikings, there were settlements of the Gaelic monks.

## Norsemen Discovery

In accord with Landnámabók, Iceland was first discovered by Naddoddr, a Viking from Faroe Island, who was sailing from Norway to the Faroe Island, but lost his way and drifted to the east coast of Iceland. Naddoddr titled the nation snæland (snowland).

## First settler

IngólfurArnarson, a Norwegian chieftain, was considered to be one of the first permanent settlers in Iceland. In 874, he and his family established their home in Reykjavik (cove of smoke).

It is believed, nevertheless, that the first permanent settler in Iceland might not just be IngólfurArnarson. There are certain grounds that suggest that it might have been one of GaròarSvavarsson's men, Náttfari, who is said to have remained behind when Garòar returned back home. Several other Norse chieftains followed suit and began to settle with their families and slaves (Thralls). These individuals mainly hailed from Norway, Scotland and Ireland. According to the Sagas of Iceland such as Landnámabók, some of the Norse chieftains' slaves were Scots and Irish.

The migration from Norway is traditionally believed to be caused by the tyranny of the king of Norway, HaraldurHárfagri, otherwise known as Harald the Fair-Haired.

## Greenland

### Norse Settlement

The existence of Greenland probably emerged in the early 10th century for Europeans. The name Greenland was coined by Eric the Red, after he discovered the land during exile from Iceland. It is recorded in historical books that *"he named the land Greenland saying that people would be eager to go there because the land has a good name."*

Erik the Red, according to the Sagas, was exiled for a period of three years for manslaughter. He sailed to Greenland and explored the coastline and claimed some regions as his own. He returned to Iceland to persuade people to join him in building a settlement on Greenland. Successful he was, as he led a fleet of 25 ships on course for Greenland. Unfortunately, only 14 made it to the destination.

It was on three separate locations the Norse settled: the larger Eastern settlement, the smaller Western settlement, and the still smaller Middle settlement (at times considered part of the Eastern one). The Norse colony in Greenland lasted for almost 500 years.

## North America

Around 986, Leif Ericson (the son of Eric the Red), þórfinnr Karlsefni and Bjarni Herjólfsson from Greenland arrived in North America and endeavored to settle in the region they Called Vinland. They generated a small-scaled settlement on the currently known Newfoundland. Unlike the colony in Greenland, the Vinland colony was abbreviated. This was due to internal conflicts with the natives and Greenland's insufficient help.

## Siege of Paris

The Vikings first attacked the Frankish empire in 799 AD. In the light of this incident, Charlemagne decided to establish a defense system along the northern coast of France, which was able to deter a Viking's attack at Seine in 820 AD. But it wasn't long before the Vikings attacked again and brought this defense system to crumbles.

From 820-840 AD Viking's raid in France wasn't as major. But then on March 845 AD, with a fleet of 120 longships and over 5000 men, the Vikings entered Seine. The army was commanded by a Danish chieftain named Ragnar Lodbrok, who was involved in the raid for retribution. As history depicts it, Ragnar was furious for the confiscation of his land in Turhot, which was given to him by Charles the Bald, successor of Charlemagne.

Ragnar's army then proceeded up the River Seine. They captivated the city of Rouen and burned it down to the ground. They assaulted, burned and looted monasteries such as the Jumiège and the Saint-Wandrille.

In response to this attack, Charles the Bald amassed an army and divided it into two parts, one for each side of the river. Ragnar's army attacked and defeated one of the smaller divisions of the Frankish army. And to incite terror, he captured 111 soldiers and hanged them on the island of Seine— the remaining forces then retreated. Then on the 28th or 29th of March, the Vikings arrived in Paris and plundered it through and through.

The Frankish forces were unable to defeat Ragnar's army, so for their withdrawal Charles the Bald offered them a payment of 2,570 kilograms of silver and gold. The Vikings took the payment and withdrew.

The Vikings raided Paris again in 860 AD, and they retired only when they were satisfied enough with what they acquired from the City. The attack inflicted upon Paris during that time was worse than the 845AD siege, but it ended up inspiring the establishment of the bridges across the Seine at Pitres and Paris, and the famous French Chivalry.

The Vikings attacked Paris again in 885AD and this time with a force larger and fiercer than ever before. The Vikings arrived with a fleet of 700 ships and as many as up to 40,000 men. It was a time in which Charles the Fat, who was already the king of Germany and Italy, acceded to power in France.

The Franks did whatever was possible to blockade the Vikings from reaching Paris, but they failed. In November 885AD, the Vikings with hundreds of ships and thousands of men managed to reach the coasts of Paris, which was then just a town in the island île de la Citè. At first the Vikings asked for payment, but then Odo, The Count of Paris, declined their request. And that was when the historical raid on Paris began.

Odo, The Count of Paris, was able to fortify the bridgehead with two towers to guard each bridge prior to the arrival of the Vikings. He was certainly prepared, but was only able to gather around 200 armed forces to safeguard the city.
On the 26th of November the Vikings activated their attacked and assailed the northeast tower with siege engines such as catapults, ballistae and mangonels. But breaking the walls of the city proved to be a futile attempt, as the Frank fought back with a fusion of pitch and hot wax, and were able to keep them at bay. During the night, when the Vikings proceeded to a river bank and camped, the Parisian erected another storey on the tower.

With renewed force and additional siege engines the Vikings continued their attack and the Franks fought back with as much force and ways as possible.  For two month this fierce battle continued, but then on February 6th 886 AD, as a result of a heavy rain, the bridge was in ruins and the northeast tower was left with only twelve guards.

The Vikings then took the tower by storm and demolished it, killing whoever roamed in its interior. They attacked the city almost on a daily basis; many were killed and much more were wounded. Seeing the anguish that rained upon the great mass, Count Odo made a covert sail and sought out help from the kingdom, alerting them that the city would come to ruins unless help arrived promptly. The emperor took notice of Odo's plea and sent out his imperial army to Paris.

The army arrived in Paris in October and did manage to disperse the Vikings. But it wasn't part of Charles' objective to go into battle with the Northmen, so he settled upon a negotiation. Upon withdrawal, Charles agreed to pay the Viking raiders 257 kilogram of gold and silver, and allowed them to sail up the River Seine and raid Burgundy without let or hindrance.

The siege of Paris by the Vikings lasted for eight months.

## The Viking Longship

One protruding element that has and still distinguishes the Vikings from any other race in medieval Europe is their invention of the longship. It was the first naval vessel ever to be built in the world and it has since served as the basis to the making of all modern naval ships.

The Vikings used their longships for commerce, exploration and warfare. Because of this longship the journey of the Vikings extended farther beyond the borders of Europe. Their expeditions included Asia Minor, the Mediterranean Sea, Northern Africa, the Arctic , even North America.

They roamed the great and daring seas of the world with command and poise, making history wherever they decided to tow their vessel. The Germans knew them as Ashmen, the Anglo-Saxons as Danes, and the Gaels called them Norse. And on the lands of the Arabs, the Byzantines and Slavs the Vikings were known as the Rus 'Rhōs'. The history of the Viking Age literally began with the formation of the longships.

The first boat bearing the design of a longship was the Umiak, and it dates back to the stone ages. The design of this boat then evolved and came to full formation between the ninth and thirteenth centuries, with vessels like the Kualsund and Nydam.

The Viking longships were all made out of wood and they each had emblematic carvings on the hull. They were double-ended, very light and had a shallow-draft hull. The engineering that went into the making of these ships permitted them to travel inland through rivers, creeks, inlet and shallow bays, which was the main reason why they triumphed in many of their raids. The average speed of the Viking Ship ranges from 5-10 knots, but it all depends on the weather condition and the type of ship that is in motion, as it can go up to about 15 knots.

## Types of Ships

The Vikings built different types of ships during that time. And they were classified according to the number of rowing positions on board, but of course their size and construction details were also put to account.

The Gulating (Thing), a 10th century legislative assemblage that convened to discuss matters involving taxation, the construction of roads and churches and military service, sketched up the labeling of these ships.

**The Karavi (Karve)** was a vessel of 13 rowing positions on board. They were mainly used for general purposes such as fishing, trade, and transportation of people or livestock. They were small Viking longships with beams of about 17 feet, so they were ideal for sails involving extremely shallow water.

There were also certain occasions where the Karavi was put to military use.
According to the Gulating, ships with 6 to 16 rowing benches were called Karavi.

**The Knarr**was an ocean-going vessel that was shorter and sturdier than the Karavi. It was used for journeys that were long and rather challenging. The name Knarr itself was a term the Norse used for ships built for Atlantic voyages. The Vikings used this ship for distant trade.

The Knarr had the capacity of traveling 121 km per day with 20-30 crew members on board. Its hull can carry up to 122 tons.

**The Skeid**is the largest longship ever used in warfare during the Viking ages. It had more than 30 rowing benches and according to the analysis of the Skeid which was discovered by Danish archeologists in Roskilde, the ship had the capacity of carrying 70-80 crew members.

**Drekkar** or **Dragon-headed** longships are probably one of the most renowned vessels in the world. Through the pages of history, these ships are described as the '13th century Göugu-Hrólfs Saga' (the Saga of Rollo).

They were warships—large, fast and used mainly to carry troops. During battle, the Vikings would sometimes tie them together to structure a stable platform. In regards to size and purpose, it has much semblance to that of the Skeid. But what made the Drekkar unique, what was captivating and incredibly interesting about this longship, was the detailed carvings of beasts and animals, such as a snake or dragon, on the prow.

Some believe that these carvings had a ritual purpose—to ward off the mythical creatures of the sea and protect the ship and crew— whereas others believed that it was purposed to frighten enemies and townsfolk.

Whatever was its purpose though, it must be acknowledged that the dragon-headed longship displayed laudable craftsmanship, especially for that era.

## Construction of the Ship

How the Vikings modeled their ships was a display of the impressive artistry that streamed in their veins. But what highlights the name of the Vikings in human history, is the engineering that went into the building of those vessels. The tools and materials they used and how they used it was most certainly advanced for people of that era.

### Tools

Viking tools have much semblance to that of those in modern days. Based on archeological findings, the Vikings used tools such as broad axe, adze, wedges, anvils, awls, snips, and different kinds of knives.

**The Augers** or (twist drill bits) were one of the most impressive Viking tools ever discovered. It had the shape of a spoon but operated much like a drilling bit. The spoon will first be fixed to a rotating shaft that's attached to a piece of curved wood. When the curved wood is then rotated with pressure applied, rivet holes come into formation.

**The broad axe** the woodworkers used was different from that of a saw or other axes used in warfare. These broad axes were used to split the trunks of trees into thin and long planks. They were also used to split the logs into wedges.

## Material

The materials used to build these historical vessels contributed a great deal to their incredible performance. These materials were actually the secret ingredients to their grandeur.

## Wood

Viking ships were light, fast and stronger than anything medieval Europe has ever seen. And such were the qualities achieved due to the strong woods that were used to construct these vessels.

According to recent analysis of timber from Viking ships, Oak was a dominating element in the making of most vessels, usually large and prestigious ones. Oak is a strong and durable timber, and when it's green, it can easily be managed by adze and axe.

It is suggested that the Vikings were more inclined to utilize Oak because of its association with Odin, the God of healing, death, knowledge, sorcery, frenzy, royalty, and the gallows in Viking mythology.

Other woods such as pine, ash elm, spruce and larch were also used. During the cold seasons, the craftsmen of the Viking ships would bury unfinished timber in the mud so as to prevent it from drying out.

## Cloth
The Vikings had a knack for sailing and the fabric they used as sail was made out of wool and linen. The sails usually had stripes of bright colors or diamond patterns. A Kerling or 'Old Woman' in Old Norse would hold the mast, which has an estimated height of about 16m, firmly. And that mast would be able to support and spread the sail as however.

Longships were able to travel faster by sail than by oars.

## Iron
Iron was barely used on Viking longships. During that period metal was very expensive and the weight they would add to the ship made them all the more undesirable. But they were still used in minimal amounts, as in to fasten the mast and the keel, to clamp two strakes (planks) together, and so forth.
Then on the later days of the Viking age, iron was used to make the ships anchor and chain.

**How Viking Ships were made**

How the ships were made depended on what its purpose was. The routine of production, however, was more or less the same.

Using an axe, the boat makers would first split the trunk of a large tree, such as Oak, and form it into long, thin planks. They would then overlap the edges of these hull planks and fasten them together with treenails— a technique called Clinker (lapstrake). To maintain a strong hull the craftsmen used waterproof caulking.

To give the ship resilience, a deck, rowing benches and a strong support for the mast, a timber floor and Crossbeams were then installed in the ship.

## Viking Navigational Technique

The Vikings were incredibly skillful when it came to navigating their ways around the great sea. So the question is, with primitive or no gear at their disposal, how were they so efficient? Well, that happens to be a question that archeologists are still unable to conclude.

However, a lot of speculations are known to surface when Viking navigational techniques are in discussion. Archeologists such as ThorkildRamskou and Leif K.Karlsen believe that the Vikings used the Sunstone for navigation. Sunstones are natural crystals that can polarize skylight. The sun's direction would be determined by the changes of color.

Whether or not the sunstone worked during a cloudy weather is still arguable.

Some archeologists believe that the Vikings made use of a Sun Compass. And the discovery of a small wooden half-disc with gnomon curves made their theory all the more plausible. The disc was discovered on the shores of Narsarsuaq, Greenland, and it is suggested that the gnomon on the center of this disc casted a shadow that helped the Viking navigator determine the direction.

## The Viking Burial Mounds

The burial of ships with deceased men and women of high social class is one of the most distinguished parts in Scandinavian culture, a tradition that dates back to 200 AD.

The Vikings believed that after death they would sail to the afterlife and join their gods in one of the nine Viking realms in Ásgard. And for the success of the journey they would be buried in their most treasured ships along with food and their valued possessions; the men with their weapons and trading tools and women with their jewelry and domestic equipment. A favored horse/horses and a faithful hunting dog were also killed and buried with the deceased. There were times where slaves were also sacrificed.

An Oseberg ship discovered in a burial mound in Norway in 1904-05 was what revealed much about Viking burial culture.

According to archeological analysis the burial mound dates back to 834 AD. And in it was found the remains of two women and several artifacts and domestic items: ornamental sleighs, wooden cart, bed-posts, wooden chests and much besides.

One of the women was dressed in a fine red woolen dress with a lozenge twill pattern and a fine linen veil, whereas the other wore a pale blue woolen dress and a woolen veil. Examinations showed that the woman dressed in red was presumably in the age range of 60-70. Her identity is still in question, but historians and researchers suggest that she might be Queen Åsa, mother of Halfdan the Black and grandmother of Harald Fairhair.

Remains of fourteen horses, one ax, and three dogs were also found in the Oseberg ship.

"When the day arrived on which the man was to be cremated and the girl with him,I went to the river on which was his ship. I saw that they had drawn the ship onto the shore, and that they had erected four posts of birch wood and other wood, and that around the ship was made a structure like great ship's tents out of wood.

Then they pulled the ship up until it was on this wooden construction Siemiradzki, Funeral of a Rus Viking Noble. One of the Rus was at my side and I heard him speak to the interpreter, who was present. I asked the interpreter what he said. He answered, "You Arabs are fools." He said "Why?" I asked him. He said, "You take the people who are most dear to you and whom you honor most and put them into the ground where insects and worms devour them. We burn him in a moment, so that he enters Paradise at once. Then he began to laugh uproariously. When I asked why he laughed, he said, "His Lord, for love of him, has sent the wind to bring him away in an hour."And actually an hour had not passed before the ship, the wood, the girl, and her master were nothing but cinders and ashes." ⍰

A 10th century Arab writer, Ahmed Ibn Fadlan, describes a Scandinavian funeral of a chieftain.

Now let's get to know the Vikings more.

## What did the Vikings look like?

The image of the Viking is often portrayed as a blond-or red-haired man of huge stature. Well, according to genetic research the Vikings were indeed blonde or red. Those from north Scandinavia— Stockholm and the surrounding areas— were predominately blond and those hailing from west Scandinavia were red-haired.

As for the depiction of their larger-than-life size, archeological findings beg to differ. According to the research conducted on the skeletons from the Viking era, their stature was much like the average human being today. The average height for men at the time was 1.73m (5ft 8 inches) and that for women was 1.57m (5ft 2 inches).

It is however correct to assume that the Vikings were physically stronger than the average man today as they were faced with tremendous physical chores in the expeditions they pursued. In truth, the Vikings were carefully selected from society. A sturdy constitution was one of the qualifications required. This was mainly because of the muscular power needed to operate the longships which depended on physical strength than wind.

Another prerequisite to becoming a Viking was an intrepid fighting skill, as many of the expeditions consisted of harrowing battles.

## The Viking Dress Code

Clothes from the Viking era are rare in discovery. The remnants found today are only rags; nevertheless, the troves of tapestries, small figures and written sources help picture a vivid image of the Viking wardrobe.

Much like today's society, age, gender, and social status established the dress code.

### Clothing of Women

Women wore strap dresses which were accompanied either by an undergarment or smock. According to research, Swedish female Vikings preferred pleated undergarments while their counterparts in Denmark opted for plain ones.The strap dresses were of coarse fabric and tight fitting. They would either be open or sewn together on the sides. Worn over the chest, the straps would be fastened with a shell-shaped brooch.

Belts with small purses would be strapped around the waist. These small pockets were used as storage for articles like a sewing needle and a strike-a-light-- which was a small piece of iron used to create fire, like a match.

Cloaks were common for the women. They would wear them over the shoulders, fastened by brooches. Between these brooches would often be a string of beads made out of silver, amber, glass or bone. They would also wear leather shoes.

## Clothing of men

A tunic, trouser and cloak would be the distinctive features that make up the male's dress code.

Little is known about the exact shape of the trousers but they might resemble plus fours.The tunic looked like a buttonless, long-armed shirt going all the way down to the knees. The cloak, fastened with brooches, was worn over the tunic. It would be gathered over the side of the arm the Viking would draw his sword or axe from— this would reveal if he was left-handed or right- handed.

Belts or strings were worn around the waist to fasten the clothes as the trousers had no elastic.

As for shoes, theywore leather boots with puttees— a sort of leg-warmer. The belt would carry knives and purses. Like the women, the men would utilize these pockets for the storage of strike-a-light, comb, silver coins, nail-cleaner and garnering pieces.

## Clothing of Children

Nothing was different about the clothing of children from the parents. The boys wore tunics and trousers; the girls wore smocks.

## Clothing of the Upper Class

The upper class of the Vikings was distinguished by the color and fabric of their attire.

The caste wore silk which was a fabric associated with wealth. The fashion was inspired by the Byzantine court style to which the elite had links to— through its association with the Christian European court class. Byzantine monopolized silk production in Europe.

Silk was a strong tool that helped flourish the power and wealth of the individual. The colors had their own significance; bright blue and red were most desired.

This class would stand out with its distinctive selection of jewelry like necklaces, elaborate brooches, belt buckles and arm rings. They would have gold threads imported from destinations as distant as Byzantium.

## The Fabric and Color of the Clothing

Troves from burials of the Viking age show that the cloths of the upper class were most certainly imported, while those of the ordinary Viking were produced locally.

Flax was an important material for fabric production; it constituted 40% of the Viking age fabric. A great deal of sites found in Denmark showed that flax was produced almost on an industrial scale. Another material used was wool. The weaving job was often left to the women.

The fabrics were woven in a variety of colors; this was made possible through the production of colored yarn which was achieved by boiling it with plants that yielded color.

According to archeological studies the colors found in the epoch were red, purple, yellow and blue. Although blue was only discovered in the burials of the elite class.

## Jewelry

Jewelry was a phenomenon favored by all levels of society and both genders. Arm rings, brooches and necklaces were worn except for earrings. Apparently, the Vikings were not so fond of them after encountering them on the Slavic during their expeditions.
Jewelry like the brooches had functional purposes—namely fastening cloths—but others had ornamental values as well as symbolic ones; they were used as a tool to show off wealth and power.

The jewelries were made of materials such as glass, wood, gold, bronze and amber. Most of them were adorned by geometric designs and heads of beasts and animals. Some would depict symbols of the god, like Thor's hammer.

## Beard and Hairstyle

The fashioning of beard and hair seemed to be an essential component in the Viking community. The discovery of numerous and various combs attests to their culture of regular combing.On the strength of certain sources, it is believed that the male Vikings styled their hair in what can be depicted as a reverse 'mullet', with long hair at the back and the top cut short.

From the artifact of a carved male head discovered at the Oseberg ship burial in Norway, it is understood that Viking men took good care of their beards. They displayed an elegant long mustache and beard.

The women were no different. Their hair was well groomed, often long and styled appealingly. Viking pendants were used to tie their hair in a bun.

## Viking Armor and weaponry

The Viking warriors were well-equipped with armor and weaponry. For protection, they used helmets, shields, and chain mails. Lance, spear, sword, axe, bow and arrow were their weapons.

Despite there being some uniformity in their weaponry, there were discrepancies in their battle dress. This was of course dependent on the social stratum the Viking belonged to and thus his economic capacity.
For the Viking with wealth and the veteran warrior, iron helmets either conically or hemispherically fashioned were exclusively available. These helmets had a bar projecting down the forehead to shield the nose.A leather body protector and a shirt of mail shielding the body from neck to knee were also accessible to those who could afford it. This protective gear was also known as a Byrine.

Axes and lances were affordable to the masses; swords, however, were exorbitant possessions of the elite.

## The health of the Vikings

Skeletal bio-archaeological studies on the Vikings show that the majority of the population— mostly ordinary farmers—suffered from arthritis of knees, back and hands. Dental bio-archaeological studies show severe dental issues. There were several teeth missing in a number of cases.Pneumonia and severely inflamed wounds were likely to have plagued the populace as well.

The Vikings lived quite a difficult life; there were a legion of battles they engaged in and most of them had fallen at these sites. The acute wounds seen on the male skeletons attest to the fierce battles they faced. Furthermore, written sources and rune stones chronicle the bloodshed and mourning of parents who had lost sons in the battles.

Life expectancy of the Vikings was relatively short. The women lived longer than the men and child mortality was high.

## Viking Homes

The largest population of the Vikings were farmers, thus most of them resided outside the towns. Their houses were surrounded by a farm encompassed by a fence, often consisting of a stable, barn and workshop.

For these Vikings, the farm, agriculture and domestic animals carried great social value. Their daily life revolved around them.

**The Longhouse:** This was a house built with wooden planks placed vertically on the ground, purposed to support the roof. Slopping posts would often be slanted on these planks from the exterior part of the house.

Damp would be a gnawing pester to these houses, eventuating in their demise but the Vikings knew how to revamp their homes. They would scorch the posts to secure longevity.

The interior design of the longhouse consisted of a long fireplace at the center which was the area where all the culinary activities were carried out. Plank-beds were built along the walls; they served the double purpose of a bed and a chair. In residences where stables were not available, the homes housed animals as well.

Since Vikings did not have windows or chimneys there was a poor ventilation system. The hole on the roof served as the only artery of ventilation; as a result the longhouseswere riddled with smoke.

Banqueting was a major social culture and as depicted in the eddic poems and the saga literature, Vikings would invite friends and neighbors to their homes to celebrate weddings, yearly festivals and funerals.Furthermore, their hospitality would extend to strangers traveling through their way; they would offer food and lodging.

Upon their death, they would be buried close to their residential areas.

## The Viking Age and Music

From parties held at the residence of a magnate to those held at the poverty-stricken farmer's home, music was a preeminent feature.

The flute and the lyre—harp-like instruments consisting of six strings—were the musical instruments employed.

As for the vocal abilities of the Vikings, the only record we have is that of the literarily accounts of the Spanish-Arabic writer Al-Tartushi. Unfortunately, it wasn't a very flattering one. After his visit to Scandinavia in the 900s, he had this to say about a song he heard in a town near the Baltic Sea: "*One hum, that was reminiscent of a dog's howl, only even more bestial.*"He claimed to have never encountered a more terrible song than that in his life. Well, they were unparalleled warriors; perhaps music wasn't their forte.

## What Were the Names Of the Vikings?

Most of the names bestowed to the Vikings emanated from the Nordic religion. Often, boys were named after the Nordic god Thor. Toke and Thorsten were common names.

Animal names like Ulf (wolf), Bjorn (bear), and Orm (serpent) were also quite popular.

Interestingly, many names used in the Viking ages are still in use today. You can find a list of the most common names and their meanings at the end of this book.

## The Social Landscape of the Vikings

Despite the savage air the Vikings projected, they were in truth a very civil populace that functioned in an orderly social landscape.

Archeological finds and the Eddic poem of Rigsthua corroborate that there were three social strata in the Viking society: Thralls, Karls, and Jarls.

**Thralls**: In essence they were slaves and had no rights. Although loathed by the others, they were an intrinsic component of the society. They shouldered the daily chores of the Vikings that were essential to a functioning society. Their responsibility ranged from tending to the farms and households of both the Jarls and Karls to the building of ramps, fortresses, mounds, roads, and many large scale productions. They were beleaguered with miserable living conditions, overloaded work and physical abuse.

There were no shortages of Thralls as the Vikings were resourceful in getting new ones. Besides those that would be born into the class—the children of the Thralls—other slaves would be supplied by the capture of new slaves they would come across during the raids. The Vikings would either bring them back to Scandinavia or have them work on new lands they settled in. At times they would trade them off to the Arabs for silver. The Slavic people of Eastern Europe were often victims of this trade. The term slave is believed to have stemmed from this area.

Slavery was a punishment for crimes like theft and murder; therefore those of a higher class could be enslaved as punitive actions against their sins.

**Karls**: Otherwise known as 'bonde' meaning free men, they can be considered the middle class of the Viking social structure. They were poor, but they were free farmers who owned land and cattle. They too would engage in daily chores and construction projects, but they would hire Thralls to lessen the burden.

**Jarls**: They were the upper class, often referred to as the magnates or chieftains. They enjoyed superiority over the other two classes and the Thralls were their slaves.

The Jarls owned large estates with farms, longhouses, domestic animals and a lot of Thralls.

They were involved in political and administrative affairs. They also engaged in sports, hunting, and expeditions to foreign land. The Jarls were responsible for mobilizing military forces for defense, battles or expeditions. The magnates were close allies of the kings and often would do their bidding.

Archeological discoveries show that household-Thralls were sometimes buried with the Jarl they belonged to.

**Kings**: The Viking society was governed by powerful kings and magnates. The title king did not carry the weight it carries today; during this era, many claimed to be kings at the same time and as a result intra fighting was rife. One did not inherit the title but fought for it.

The king was basically the leading magnate, regarded by the class as 'first among equals.' He would have body guards and a personal army—the housekarls. Besides his preeminent priority of protecting his kingdom, the king's role revolved around amassing military power and leading them to expeditions and returning with telling results.

Warriors were recruited from respected families of the Viking society. The free farmers or Karls would also serve as warriors.

Pseudo parliaments like the Thing were among the institutions which would set order and curtail social unrest.

## Women of the Viking Age

Surprisingly, the Viking women enjoyed more liberty than elsewhere in their period. The troves of written sources paint very independent women with certain rights. This, however, doesn't mean that the women had equal opportunities or rights amongst the society. They were inferior to the men, forbidden to appear in court or claim rights to shares of the man's inheritance.

They did,however, have some rights to choose their marital partner and to request for a divorce. In demanding a divorce a few factors played into the equation. Common reasons for a divorce were domestic violence and an abrupt poverty of the man's family. A woman had the right to demand for a divorce if her husband chose to settle elsewhere.

Adultery was severely punishable for women; however, the men had full liberty to even invite his mistresses to his home.

The majority of the women were housewives that took full control of the farm and house when the husbands would set out to expeditions. Their responsibilities involved housekeeping, cooking, weaving, working wool and spinning yarn.

It's probable that there were female entrepreneurs. Archeological finds show that women were involved in the production of fabric while the men were assigned to carpentry and metal work.

## Language

So far, the only literary troves of the Viking age before the introduction of Christianity are the inscriptions on rune stones.

The Vikings were literate and their alphabets were known as runors. The rune stones have helped bring us closer to them; they were often built as a tribute to the dead and had inscriptions with the name and a brief chronicle of the Viking's history. These artifacts, largely found in Scandinavia, show the destinations the Vikings had traveled to: Greece, England, Jerusalem and much besides.

## The Nordic Religion

Because of their bohemian religion, the Vikings were known to the Christians as 'the heathens from hell.' Before the advent of Christianity, the only religion known to them was the Nordic religion.

The Elder Edda (Poetic Edda) and the Younger Edda (Prose Edda) are the books relating the Nordic Myths authored by SnorriSturluson. These books along with rune stones, sladic poetry, and depictions written by Christians and Arabic travelers are sources of the Nordic religion.Archeological discoveries have also attested to early belief of the Vikings and their gods.

# The Nordic Gods

Ásgard was the home of the gods which constituted nine realms; it is a huge garrisoned castle that floats in the air. The Viking idea of heaven is known as Valhalla (home of the slain); it is the place where warriors who had fallen to battles would go. Midgard is the earth with its human dwellers and Æsir is a collective term for the Nordic gods and goddesses.

The arch-nemesis of the Æsir and humans existed at the rear end of the universe; they were known as the giants. Although they were related to the Nordic gods, they often waged war against them and Thor was the god that would go hunting for them.

The pantheon of gods each had various dispositions, weaknesses, and strengths. They carry traits of human beings and can appear as one. They were much respected and regular sacrificial ceremonies had to be carried out to avoid their wrath. An apocalyptic endwas prophesied, where the gods, humans, and giants would meet at in a final battle—the Ragnarök.

Below is a list of the most deified gods.

## Odin

He was the supreme god of the Norse pantheons and the ruler of Valhalla. Through the Valkyries (choosers of the slain)—his handmaidens— he would gather the souls of warriors killed in battles and bring them to Valhalla. They would then feast there and prepare for the ultimate war of Ragnarök.

Although Odin initially started off as the god of death, his reign extended to magic—namely runic magic—battle grounds, poetry, healing and the fury berserk-warrior. To reach this reign, Odin had to make quite a few sacrifices. He sacrificed his one eye to Mimir to drink from the source of wisdom, the well of Mimir; he was thus one-eyed and wore an eye patch. He also sacrificed himself by hanging on Yggdrasil, the world tree, and piercing himself with his own spear to master the arts of runic magic.

Odin was most worshiped by the Kings, warriors, chieftains and his men.He is served by the two ravens Huggin and Munnin and the two wolves Ferki and Geri. Slepnir is the eight legged horse he owns.

## Thor

He is the most celebrated Æsir and is known as the god of war, thunderstorm and fertility. Equipped with his hammer Mjöllnir, magic belt and iron glove, he would fight the giants fiercely. He travelled with a chariot pulled by the two goats Tanngnjóstr and Tanngrisni and would unleash thunder as he makes his way through the clouds.
He is the son of Odin but his traits differ from his father's. Unlike Odin who is unpredictable, Thor is trusted and comprehensible, he upheld law and order.

## Loki

He is originally of a giant blood but he resides in Ásgard. Notorious for his cunning disposition, Loki was disliked by the other gods, but he was, nonetheless, tolerated because he was Odin's half-brother.

Loki loathed and hated the Æsir and would often deceive both them and the giants and incite fights between them. His cunning abilities were exhibited when he convinced the equally sly dwarves to smith different magical objects of the gods—particularly Thor'sMjöllnir.

## Frey (Freyr)

Frey is distinguished by his magical boar Gullinborsts, which glistens like gold and travels on land and water faster than any horse.
Frey is the god of vegetation, harvest, wealth and peace. He is the twin brother of Freyja.

## Freyja (Freya)

Blessed with a beauty superior to all the female Æsir, she is deified as the goddess of love, fertility, and the practice of Seid.

## Sacrifices

The Nordic gods held a very essential influence over the daily lives of the Vikings and their various battles, thus sacrifices of all kinds, including human sacrifices, were made in respect to these gods. These rituals were mostly held at the residents of magnates.

Human sacrifices were the most valuable kinds and sources show that Odin demanded them.

An archeological finding of these sacrificial sites at Trellborg found five wells in which skeletons of humans and animals were discovered. From the five human relics four were children between the ages of four and five.

The finding of these sacrifices near wells corroborates the symbolic significance the Vikings had for wells; after all, Odin sacrificed his one eye to drink from the well of Mimir in exchange for wisdom.

## Viking Legends

When it comes to legendary warriors, no one in Europe can count as many as that of the Scandinavians. The Vikings were great warriors, explorers and raiders, making the Viking Age one of the most extraordinary and interesting part of human history. And had it not been for those legends who marshaled those historical pursuits, none of it would have occurred.

### Ragnar Lodbrok

Ragnar Lodbrok or **'Reginherus'**, in Old Norse, was a Danish chieftain who initiated the famous raid in France in 845AD and acquired 2570 kilograms of silver and gold. It was this and many other raids and conquests that made Ragnar a Viking hero and eventually a Norse ruler. Not much of Ragnar's private life has been chronicled, but according to several sagas, he was married three times, and fathered many sons; some of who were historical figures themselves, Ivar the Boneless, BjörnIronside, HalfdanRagnarsson, Sigurd Snake-in-the-Eye, and Ubba. On the word of these legends, Ragnar was captured by King Ælla of Northumbria and executed by venomous snakes. His sons avenged his death by besieging England with the Great Heathen Army.

## Erik Thorvaldsson

Erik Thorvaldsson otherwise known as **Eric the Red** was the first person to discover and establish a Norse settlement in Greenland. Eric's expedition to Greenland began when he was sentenced to exile for manslaughter. According to the Norse's saga, the conflict that ended in murder was initiated over Setsstorkkr, ornamental beams which were believed to have mystical powers. When Erik moved to the island of Öxney (Iceland) to build his house, he asked Thorgest to keep his valued Setsstorkkr, which he inherited from his father. But on his return, Erik's request was denied.

Devastated and outraged, Erik stormed in Thorgest's house and took it back, not much detail is provided to clarify this section. But it was stated that Erik slaughtered two of Thorgest's sons when they confronted him. It was then the Thing or Gulatpins, sentenced Eric to three years in exile.

Erick then sailed up to unknown islands and eventually found Greenland. He spent those three years of exile exploring this mysterious land. And after he served his time of punishment, he went back to Iceland and persuaded people to join him in the quest of colonizing Greenland.

Part of his persuasive method was naming this mysterious land 'Greenland'. *"People would be attracted to go there if it had a favorable name"* he explained. And he did manage to get the support he needed, but of the 400-500 of his followers only 350 survived the journey.

Erik the Red had four children with his wife Thjodhildr: Freydís, þorvaldr(Thorvald),þorsteinn (Thorstein), and the famous explorer LeifEricsson, who went on to become the first Viking to sail up to North America.
One fun fact; the name 'Eric the Red' was inspired by his red hair and beard.

## Bjorn Ironside

Bjorn Ironside, son of Ragnar Lodbrok, was a Viking chieftain and naval commander, who rose to the glories of fame after his legendary raid on Rome.
At first, in the spirit of following in his father's footstep Bjorn, accompanied by his brother Hastein, raided the north of France in 860 AD. But then the brothers, deciding to further their expeditions of the Mediterranean, relinquished their quest of returning back home to Norway and continued their sail. They raided the Spanish coastal, passed through the Straits of Gibraltar and made it all the way to the South of France, where they dwelt for the winter.

On the following year, Bjorn headed for Pisa, a city where he heard of the great riches harbored in the Holy City of Rome. Thinking that it was just a short journey inland, they began their sail to Rome. After arriving in the town of

Luna, Bjorn and his army began their siege, thinking that they had reached Rome. It was an unsuccessful attempt, as the Vikings were unable to break through the city wall. Understanding the strength of his opponent, Bjorn crafted a plot that granted him entry. Bjorn had a message sent to the Bishop of Luna saying that he had died with a final wish of being buried in the holy ground of the Christian church. The Bishop allowed the entry of Bjorn's body along with a small honor guard. Once the coffin entered the church, Bjorn leaped out and with the assistance of the honor guard headed towards the town gates and allowed his army to enter. The raid of Rome was one of Bjorn's legendary raids.

## Harald Hardrada

Harald Hardrada(Hardrada, meaning 'stern ruler' in Old Norse) was the legendary Viking warrior and king of Norway from 1046-1066 AD.

Harald first embarked upon the path of a warrior when he joined Olaf Haraldsson (Saint Olaf), his half-brother, in the Battle of Stiklestad at just the age of fifteen. It was the battle in which Olaf toiled to regain the throne of Norway back from Cnut the Great, the Danish king. The attempt was a massive failure, one that resulted in Harald facing years of exile.

During his fifteen years of exile, Harald became a captain of the army of Grand Prince Yaroslav the Wise, in

KievanRus', and later, a commander of the Byzantine Varangian Guard in Constantinople. Harald acquired a considerable amount of military experience and wealth during his years in Constantinople.

Then in 1042 Harald returned to KievanRus' and began to initiate his preparation for battle to regain the Norwegian throne.

Assuming that the throne was passed down from the Dannish to Olaf's son, Mangnus the Good, Harald allied with SweynEsstridsson, Mangus' rival. The alliance, however, was short-lived when Mangus refused to engage in a battle with his uncle and sought out an agreement that suited both parties – Mangus reached a resolution to share his empire with Harald, and Harald his riches with him.

Then on the following year this partnership came to an end, when Mangus succumbed and Harald ended up becoming Norway's sole ruler.

Great economic strides were seen in Norway during Harald's reign; he outlined the territorial unification of the country under national governance, instituted a viable coin and foreign trade.
Harald never abandoned his quest to claim the Danish throne. And though he prospered in many of his raids, never was he able to defeat Denmark. He also made notable attempts to assume the throne of England in 1066.

He attacked the borders of northern England and successfully defeated the regional army in the Battle of Fulford. But then in the Battle of Stamford Bridge, Harald was overcome and slaughtered by King Harold Godwinson's army.

According to historians, the death of Harald at the Battle of Stamford Bridge marked the conclusion of the Viking Era.

## Debunking the Myths

Many incorrect perceptions continue to distort the image and perception of the Vikings, so let's start debunking those myths.

**The Vikings wore horned helmets.**
*There is no evidence suggesting that Vikings wore such an elaborate headgear. Archeological finds show that most of them went bear head or wore leather headgear with wood. The privileged cast wore simple round metal helmets but nothing extravagant.*

*From a pragmatic point of view, it wouldn't have made sense for them to have worn such a cumbersome gear as they often fought at close quarters. It would not have only posed as an impediment, but a danger as well.*

**Vikings had a savage appearance, wild-hair and wild-eyes.**
*Countless combs, ear picks, and tweezers kept securely in boxes were found by archeologists. This corroborates the fact that hygiene and appearance really mattered to the*

*Vikings. And given that regular combing was a custom of theirs, the theory of a wild-hair look seems a touch out of balance.*

*Moreover, the Anglo-Saxon neighbors of the Anglo-Danes who settled in Great Britain claimed that they bathed weekly and groomed their hair well.*

**Vikings played the lure.**
*No they did not.*

**Vikings drank out of skulls.**
*No they did not. No evidence to support this.*

**The only weapons Vikings used in battles were axes.**
*Not true. They had swords, bows and arrows, spears and laces. Artifacts of the Viking age found in graves, lakes, battle fields, and ford attest to this fact.*

**Vikings were buried in dolmen.**
*Not true either.*

# List of Viking Names

## Male names from the Viking Age

**Arne**: eagle
**Birger**: keeper
**BjØrn**: bear
**Frode**: wise and clever
**Bo**: the resident
**Njal**: giant
**Gorm**: he who worships god
**Erik**: absolute ruler
**Halfdan**: the half Danish
**Harald**: lord and ruler
**Knud**: knot
**Kåre**: with curly hair
**Leif**: descendant
**Roar**: fame and spear
**Rune**: secret
**Sten**: stone
**Skarde**: with cleft chin
**Sune**: son
**Svend**: freeman who is in the service of another
**Troels**: Thor's arrow
**Toke**: Thor and helmet
**Torsten**: Thor and stone
**Trygve**: trustworthy
**Ulf**: wolf
**Ødger**: wealth and spear

# Female names from the Viking Age

**Astrid**: beautiful, loved
**Bodil**: penance and fight
**Frida**: peace Gertrud: spear
**Gro**: to grow
**Estrid**: god and beautiful
**Hilda**: the fighter
**Gudrun**: god and rune
**Gunhild**: fight
**Helga**: sacred
**Inga**: of the god
**Inge** Liv: of life
**Randi**: shield or shrine
**Signe**: the one who is victorious
**Sigrid**: victorious horsewoman
**Revna**: raven
**Sif**: wife and bride
**Tora**: of the god Thor
**Tove**: dove
**Thyra**: helpful
**Thurid**: Thor and beautiful
**Yrsa**: wild or she bear
**Ulfhild**: wolf or battle

# Conclusion

It is evident that the Viking age is an essential part of history, and that the Viking society is clearly more than the ferocious horde it has been thought to be. To the contrary, they were an innovative and civil society that functioned in an orderly system.

The turbulent and perplex relic of the Viking age makes the epoch all the more fascinating, and it is the thrust of this book to satisfy all curiosity and debunk the rife misconceptions.

Printed in Great Britain
by Amazon